Colli

Tr sh

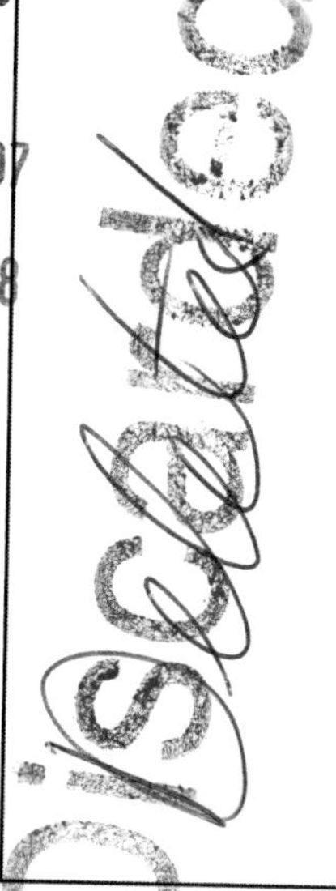

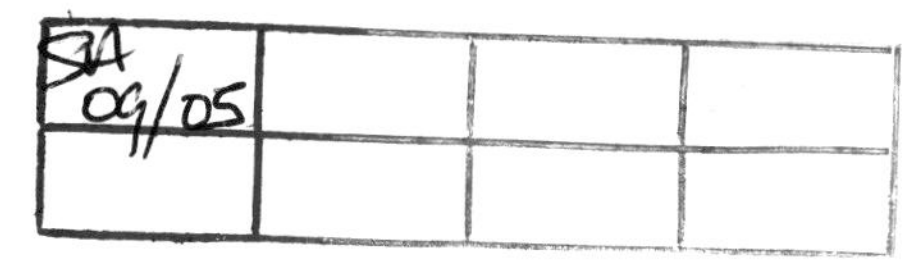

New 3rd Edition
First published in 2005 by
Collins, an imprint of
HarperCollins*Publishers*
77-85 Fulham Palace Road
Hammersmith, London W6 8JB

The Collins website is www.**collins**.co.uk

10 09 08 07 06 05
10 9 8 7 6 5 4 3 2 1

First published as *Care for your Tropical Fish* in 1986 by
William Collins Sons & Co Ltd, London

Second edition published in 1990

Reprinted by
HarperCollins*Publishers*
and subsequently reprinted 13 times

The RSPCA is a registered charity (no. 219099)
The RSPCA website is www.rspca.org.uk

Designed by: SP Creative Design
Editor: Heather Thomas
Design: Rolando Ugolini

Photographs
Alamy: pages 6 (Robert Harding Picture Library Ltd), 7 and 33 (Maximilian Weinzier)
Juwel Aquariums: page 21 (provided by Just Buy Online t/a The Aquarium Shop)
Photomax UK: pages 5, 26, 39, 46
Practical Fishkeeping Magazine: page 27
www.jjphoto.dk: page 17

A catalogue record for this book is available from the British Library

ISBN 0 00 719359 9

Colour reproduction by Colourscan
Printed and bound by Printing Express, Hong Kong

Foreword

Owning tropical fish is great fun but a huge responsibility. All animals need a regular routine and lots of love and attention, but most importantly, pets need owners who are going to stay interested in them and committed to them all their lives.

Anyone who has ever enjoyed the company of a pet knows just how strong the bond can be. Children learn the meaning of loyalty, unselfishness and friendship by growing up with animals. Elderly or lonely people often depend on a pet for company and it has been proved that animals can help in the prevention of and recovery from physical or mental illness.

The decision to bring a pet into your home should always be discussed and agreed by everyone in the family. Bear in mind that parents are ultimately responsible for the health and well-being of the animal for the whole of its lifetime. If you are not prepared for the inevitable expense, time, patience and occasional frustration involved, then the RSPCA would much rather that you didn't have a pet.

Being responsible for a pet will completely change your life but if you make the decision to go ahead, think about offering a home to one of the thousands of animals in RSPCA animal centres throughout England and Wales. There are no animals more deserving of loving owners.

As for the care of your fish, this book should provide you with all the information you need to keep them happy and healthy for many years to come. Enjoy the experience!

Steve Cheetham MA, VetMB, M[illegible]
Chief Veterinary Officer, RSPCA

Introduction

The first public aquarium in the world was opened in England in 1852, in the Zoological Gardens in Regent's Park, London, and since then, keeping and breeding tropical fish has increased in popularity enormously. The wide range of species and colours make them fascinating to own and relaxing to watch as they glide silently through the plants in the home aquarium.

Tropical fish can be divided into two categories: freshwater and marine fish. This book is concerned only with freshwater tropical fish. The requirements for marine fish tend to be complex and demand considerable expertise, as well as more time, effort and money than the newcomer to fish keeping will wish to expend.

That said, keeping freshwater fish as pets still requires certain basic commitments on the part of the owner. Fish are living creatures and although they cannot show their feelings as demonstratively as cats or dogs, they still need to be well looked after if they are to thrive.

Many hundreds of brightly coloured tropical freshwater fish are readily available from aquarist shops. It is worth taking the time to investigate different species and to acquire a little basic knowledge in order to ensure a congenial and healthy environment for your fish which will make your aquarium a source of living interest and delight. You will come to appreciate their complex behaviour and how they interact.

▼ The black and silver stripes of the Angelfish and Black Widow Tetras complement each other and provide a contrast to the bright colours of the Neon Tetras.

Freshwater fish in the tropics

Tropical freshwater fish come from many different habitats around the world, which range from the fast-flowing mountain streams of China to the huge inland freshwater lakes of Africa, especially the Rift Valley.

Africa

Both Africa and South America have their fair share of three popular, often specialized, groups of fishes – the cichlids, catfish and killifish.

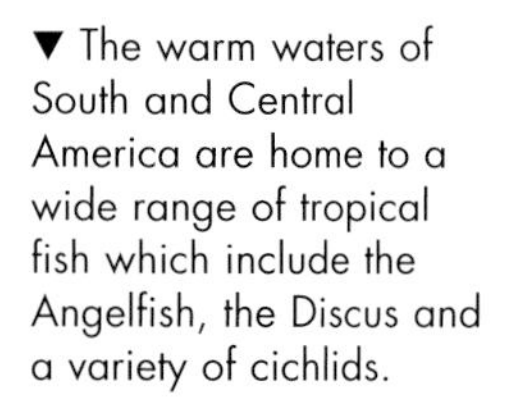

▼ The warm waters of South and Central America are home to a wide range of tropical fish which include the Angelfish, the Discus and a variety of cichlids.

Central and South America

Most live-bearing fish, such as Guppies, Swordtails, Platies and Mollies, are native to the Central Americas, where they are inhabitants

of waterways which often receive some tidal waters. Colourful tetras are perennial aquarium favourites; the diminutive Neon and Cardinal Tetras are closely related to the Piranha and share its South American watercourses along with other aquarium favourites, the Angelfish and Corydoras Catfish.

▲ A mouth breeding cichlid will incubate fertilized eggs in its mouth for about three weeks before releasing the young fry.

India and South-east Asia

The slow-moving rivers of India and South-east Asia are the home of Rasboras and Barbs, whilst the graceful Gouramis and the belligerent Siamese Fighting Fish are able to survive often oxygen-depleted waters by virtue of their auxilliary breathing organs.

Biology

Scales Externally, the body of the fish is covered with some small bony plates – scales – which are themselves covered with a delicate layer of skin (although this is usually too thin to be seen without a microscope) which enlarges the scales as the fish grows. On top of this is a layer of mucus with bactericidal properties. The scales can only protect the fish by growing. If the delicate skin is damaged, growth is affected, so the fish's well-being is put at risk. For this reason, extreme care must be taken when handling fish – it is better not to handle them at all if possible. If too much mucus is removed by handling, bacteria can get into the skin and set up an infection; if too much skin is removed, the scales cannot grow; and if the scales cannot grow, the fish can lose body fluids or become infected and die.

Gills Most fish breathe by taking in water through the mouth, which then closes, the muscles squeezing the water out through the slits in the side of the throat. The bars between the slits are lined with delicate blood-filled filaments (gill filaments), which act like our lungs. They pick up oxygen from the water and remove the carbon dioxide from the fish's blood. The gills nestle below a large protective plate just behind the head, which is called the gill cover, or operculum.

Barbels Some fish, notably bottom-dwelling species such as catfish and loaches, have 2–6 whiskery growths around the mouth; these 'barbels' are equipped with taste and touch cells, enabling the fish to locate food in dark, murky waters.

Eyes Fish have no eyelids, so those kept in an aquarium need to be shaded from direct sunshine.

Dorsal fin This fin may have spiny rays in front or may be made up entirely of soft rays. It acts as a keel to stabilize the fish and, if it is brightly marked, may be rather like a signalling flag, helping to keep shoals together. It can also be used to 'warn' other species.

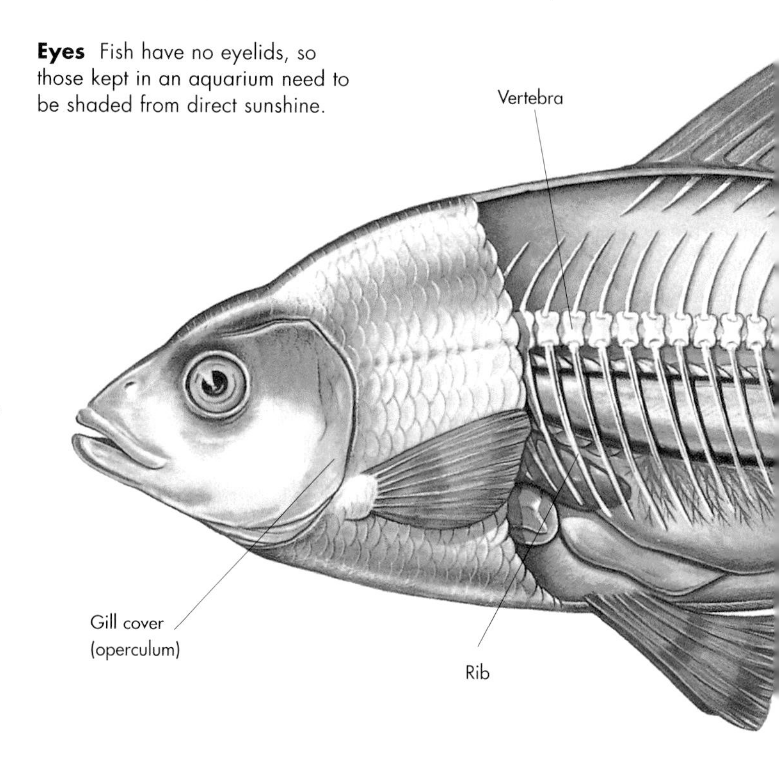

Pectoral fins Just behind the operculum are the pectoral fins, which are the fish's equivalent of arms. Like the pelvic fins, they help the fish to brake and steer.

Pelvic fins The paired fins in front of the anal fin are called the pelvic fins. These fins help the fish with braking and steering.

Fins Fins are the most conspicuous features of a fish and are of great help in determining to which group of fish your specimen belongs. As well as having various locomotory functions, they can serve many other purposes, as described here.

Swim bladder Many fish (most of the ones that you are likely to encounter) have a large gas- or air-filled sac, which is variously called the swim bladder, gas bladder or air bladder. This is not usually used for breathing. It acts as a buoyancy chamber to keep the fish at the required depth in the water without effort. It uses its swim bladder to make itself neutrally buoyant.

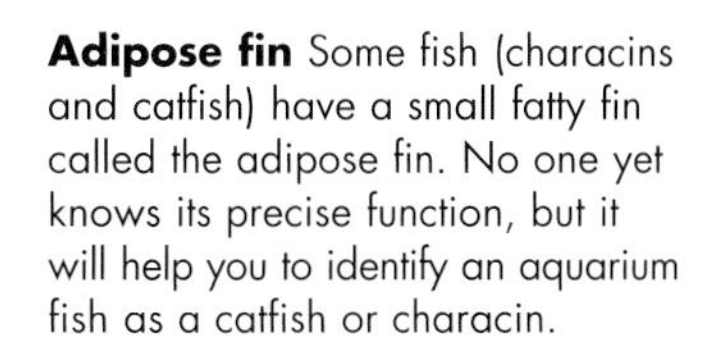

Adipose fin Some fish (characins and catfish) have a small fatty fin called the adipose fin. No one yet knows its precise function, but it will help you to identify an aquarium fish as a catfish or characin.

Caudal fin At the end of the body is the caudal or tail fin, which can be one of a variety of shapes. In the male swordtail, the lower rays of the caudal fin are elongated into the colourful sword that gives these species their common name. The tail imparts the thrust of the side-to-side movements which make the fish go forwards.

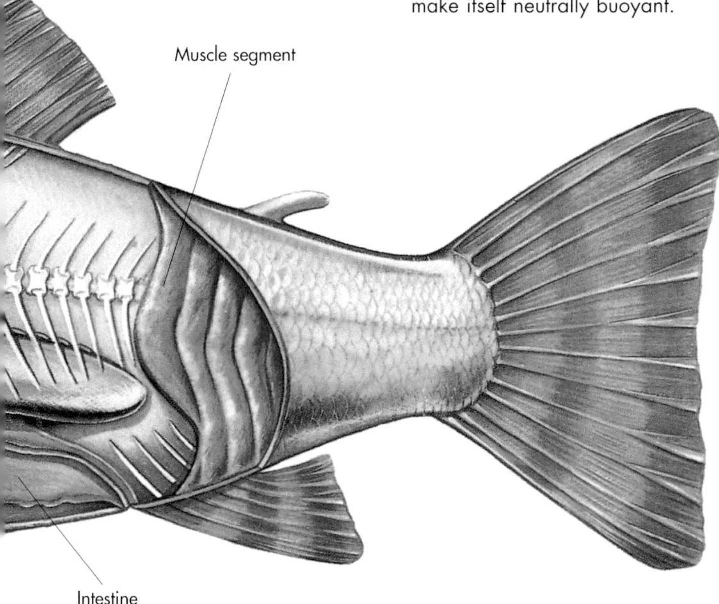

Anal fin On the underside of the body, just behind the anus, is the anal fin. Like the dorsal fin, it acts as a stabilizer, except in the males of live-bearing species where it is used in reproduction. For example, in fish like Guppies and Swordtails, the anal fin of the male is modified into a rod-like structure to transfer the sperm to the female.

Lateral line Running down the side of many fish is a line, which is called the lateral line, and it is formed by a series of pores in a row of scales. These pores lead to a canal with pressure-sensitive organs. The lateral line system acts like a sense of 'distant touch', which can alert the fish to many obstacles and dangers.

Fish for the aquarium

Choosing a selection of fish

It is a good idea to choose a selection of fish that live at varying depths (surface, middle-water and bottom levels), thereby maximizing all your available tank space. To obtain both an aesthetic and 'ecological' balance, fish should be chosen to suit these areas although most, at some time or another, will visit areas other than those allocated to them.

To illustrate such a distribution, Danios and Rasboras are active surface area fish constantly on the move; the longer-finned Angelfish and Gouramis are much slower in their movements, living happily in mid-water amongst the tall grassy plants accompanied by the decorative Tetras and constantly foraging Barbs. Bottom-dwelling fish, such as many Catfish, are often nocturnal by nature and will spend the daytime hours (or when the tank is artificially lit) hidden among the rocks and plants waiting for 'night' to fall.

Live-bearing fish, although having the upturned mouths of surface feeders, seem to occupy any level they feel like in the aquarium. We shall therefore describe these 'non-conformists' first.

▲ Male Guppy (*Poecilia reticulata*)

The Guppy *(Poecilia reticulata)*

The many colourful strains of the Guppy are internationally recognized; its alternative common name of Millions Fish also confirms its readiness to breed. The sexes are easily distinguished as the females, although they are much larger than the males, are less brightly patterned. The Guppy is a shoaling fish and one of the most popular choices for the aquarium, being attractive, inexpensive and easy to keep.

The Swordtail *(Xiphophorus helleri)*

Green when found in the wild in Central America, this distinctive fish has been bred in red, black and many mixed colours. It grows to about 9 cm (3½ in) long. The long extension to the bottom of the male's caudal fin makes the Swordtail instantly recognizable, but sex-reversal (female to male) is not uncommon in adult Swordtails.

Feeding tip

Make sure that you always include plenty of green matter in all live-bearers' diets (see pages 36–37).

◀ The distinctive Green Swordtail (*Xiphophorus helleri*) has an extension to the bottom of the male's caudal fin (left).

◀ The colourful Platy (*Xiphophorus maculatas*) is plump with a short, compact tail (far left).

The Platy *(Xiphophorus maculatus)*

The Platy is a peaceful, sociable fish which comes in a wide range of colours; even the females are brightly coloured. Its preferred water temperature is probably 24–26°C (75–80°F) and the aquarium should be well lit to encourage algae growth. Platies can be reliable breeders.

The Molly *(Poecilia spp.)*

These popular live-bearers can be green and gold spotted or all black, depending on which species you choose.

▼ These Mollies (*Poecilia velifera*) are swimming through some typical aquarium plants.

Surface feeders

All the fish that are found 'just under the surface' have a perfectly straight back, which allows their upturned mouths (ideal for scooping up floating foods – usually insects in nature) to get right up to the surface. Foods that float for some time are ideal for these fish.

▲ The Zebra Danio (*Brachydanio rerio*) is a hardy fish with attractive zebra-like stripes.

The Zebra Danio *(Brachydanio rerio)*

A native of India, this fish enjoys a water temperature of between 20°C (68°F) and 23°C (73°F). A very active and lively fish, it will reach a size of about 5 cm (2 in) and is best kept in shoals. Females are much plumper than males. For novices, the Zebra Danio may be regarded as an ideal fish with which to begin breeding; the parents should be removed as soon as possible after spawning as they love eating their own eggs. Alternatively, use dense bunches of plants in which the eggs can lodge well out of their reach.

The Glass Catfish *(Kryptopterus bicirrhis)*

This almost transparent fish – you can see its bones – has a single ray for a dorsal fin (see page 24). It originates in South-east Asia, growing easily to about 10 cm (4 in) long. It enjoys a temperature range of 21–26°C (70–80°F). As it is an active, free-swimming, shoaling fish, don't keep just one; otherwise it may pine away. Unlike most other catfish, it spends quite a lot of time in the upper levels of the water.

The Silver Hatchetfish

(Gasteropelecus sternicla)

▲ Silver Hatchetfish (*Gasteropelecus sternicla*)

The very deep body of this species from South America houses powerful muscles which 'flap' the pectoral fins as it leaps above the surface to chase insects or escape predators. A covered tank is essential for this family of fish if it is not to end up on the carpet. A peaceful shoaling species, it is best kept in groups of six or more. They seem to prefer warmer water than most tropicals, within a range of 23–30°C (73–86°F).

The Siamese Fighting Fish *(Betta splendens)*

This is a hardy fish, but you can keep only one male in a tank or fighting will break out. If you want to see it display, put a mirror at the side of the tank. When a female is present, the male fish blows a nest of bubbles under which to spawn and guard the floating eggs. Aquarium-cultivated strains usually have bodies and fins of one colour, which may be bright red, blue or green, but the 'Cambodia' Fighter (also aquarium-developed) has a cream body with coloured fins.

▲ The spectacular Siamese Fighting Fish (*Betta splendens*) needs a quiet tank as it can be bullied by fin nippers, and have its fins damaged.

Butterfly Fish *(Pantodon buchholzi)*
A native of the Zaire region of Africa, the Butterfly Fish will hang motionless beneath the surface of the water for long periods, waiting for insects to alight above it. Like the Hatchetfish, it can leap out of the water to glide for some distance, using its out-spread pectoral fins, although it does not actually 'flap' them.

Incidentally, it is not until you look down on this fish from above the tank that you realize the significance of its common name – the pectoral fins are like butterfly wings. It is the only species in its genus and may be predacious towards small fishes.

◀ These Butterfly Fish (*Pantodon buchholzi*) get their name from their pectoral fins which look like a butterfly's wings.

Midwater feeders

Easily identified by their terminal mouths situated right on the front of the snout, midwater swimmers and feeders form the largest group of fish in the aquarium and offer you an almost limitless choice.

All are normal 'fish-shaped', with the dorsal and anal contours being similarly convex. However, the disc-shaped Angelfish and Discus are slower-moving fish, and their narrow bodies enable them to slip between the tank plants effortlessly.

Angelfish *(Pterophyllum scalare)*

The disc-shaped body of the Angelfish is not representative of the cichlid family, but this South American fish is still an all-time aquarium favourite. The original wild species had a silver body with dark vertical bars, but there are now marbled, gold, albino and even 'blushing' varieties with exaggerated fin lengths, all of which have been produced in the Far East by selective breeding. Angelfish make a graceful addition to the aquarium but, if large, may harass other smaller fish. Well-matched, self-selected pairs breed easily and look after their young.

▲ Angelfish (*Pterophyllum scalare*)

The Cardinal Tetra *(Paracheirodon axelrodi)*

This brilliantly coloured fish from South America is not only related to the Piranha but also has just as many teeth. At 3 cm (1 in), it is similar in size to the Neon Tetra (*P. innesi*) but is easily distinguishable – the Neon has only a half-length red band on the body.

The Glowlight Tetra *(Hemigrammus erythrozonus)*

A delicately glowing reddish-gold line shines along the sides of the body and the top of the eye is red. This fish is seen at its best in a well-planted tank with a dark bottom covering.

▶ The iridescent red stripe of the Glowlight Tetra (*Hemigrammus erythrozonus*) shines as though lit from within.

The Harlequin Fish *(Rasbora heteromorpha)*

This lively but peaceful Rasbora enjoys being in shoals, when all the fish move as one. It will thrive on a diet of flaked fish-food and grows to a size of about 4.5 cm ($1^{3}/_{4}$ in). The Harlequin Fish appreciates soft, acid water. It lays its eggs on the undersides of broad-leaved plants.

▲ The Harlequin Fish (*Rasbora heteromorpha*) is a good choice for a community aquarium as it likes being in shoals.

The Ruby Barb *(Barbus nigrofasciatus)*

The Ruby Barb is so called because the colour of the male fish undergoes a remarkable change at breeding time. The whole body is suffused with rich red-purple, especially so in the head region; the female remains a dark-striped pale yellow fish. These barbs grow to about 5 cm (2 in) in length and are very active fish. You should supplement their flaked food with some live food, such as Daphnia and worms.

Pearl Gourami

(Trichogaster leeri)

This very pretty fish is generally peaceful but is sensitive to bad water conditions. Best kept in pairs, they reach a size of about 10 cm (4 in). They enjoy subdued light and will build floating bubble nests in which they place their eggs.

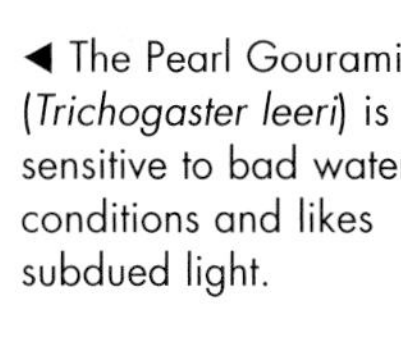

◀ The Pearl Gourami (*Trichogaster leeri*) is sensitive to bad water conditions and likes subdued light.

The Tiger Barb

(Barbus tetrazona)

This aquarium favourite from the Far East grows to around 5 cm (2 in) and it is easily recognized by its four dark bands and the red-orange edges to the fins. If it is kept in small numbers, it may nip the fins of slower-moving fish, but keeping a shoal of Tiger Barbs may help to solve this problem.

◀ The Tiger Barb (*Barbus tetrazona*) can be quite aggressive to other fish so never put a solitary one in your aquarium as it will pick on the other inhabitants. Always keep them in a large group so that they quarrel with each other and ignore any other fish.

Bottom-dwelling species

Not unexpectedly, bottom-swimming species have physical characteristics that are almost the opposite of surface-swimming fish. Their ventral (lower) contour is flat, allowing their mouths, which are often adorned with barbels, to get as near as possible to the bottom in order to seek out and pick up food. Their flat-bottomed bodies mean they will not be lifted off the bottom by fast-flowing water currents and swept away.

Some Catfish, whilst not being entirely bottom-dwelling, have sucker mouths for rasping algae from rocks; the Chinese Sucking 'Loach' (*Gyrinocheilus aymonieri*), which is not a loach nor does it come from China, has a special hole in the upper gill cover in order to breathe without releasing its 'sucker-hold' on a rock. Adults may attack other fish.

Scavengers

South America and Africa are both excellent natural sources of large numbers of aquarium-suitable Catfish, and some aquarists specialize in these fish. They are one of the largest and most varied of all fish families with over 2,000 species. Many hobbyists tend to regard the bottom-dwelling fish as scavengers, expecting them to thrive on food left over by other fish. While many Catfish do obtain their food this way, they should not be denied food in their own right, and feeding fast-sinking, or tablet foods (especially last thing at night) will do much to ensure that these fish get their rightful share of proper foods.

The Bronze Catfish *(Corydoras aeneus)*

Catfish of this shoaling genus have no scales – their skin is covered by two rows of overlapping bony plates, which are called scutes. Another characteristic physical feature they possess is the ability to rotate each eye independently in the socket. An 'albino' form of this fish has been aquarium-developed.

▶ The Bronze Catfish (*Corydoras aeneus*) is unusual in having no scales. Its body is covered in bony plates called scutes.

The Peppered Catfish *(Corydoras paleatus)*
Like the preceding species, the Peppered Catfish is also a longstanding aquarium favourite. Many corydoras are relatively easy to breed by the addition of some cold water to their aquarium. This simulates their natural conditions where melted ice-waters enter their South American river systems each spring and trigger breeding. During spawning, the female corydoras carry the fertilized eggs between their pelvic fins to a hatching site, usually on plant leaves or the aquarium glass.

The Pleco *(Hypostomus plecostomus)*
Usually purchased for its algae-removing services, the Suckermouth Catfish, or Pleco, should continue to be given green foods once it has completed its allotted task if it is to thrive. Vegetable matter forms an essential part of this fish's diet, and the addition of lettuce, spinach leaves and green peas will be much appreciated.

Placing your aquarium in a sunny location will help to encourage the growth of algae, and fortunately, the fish is not discomforted by any bright light; it can adjust the level of light entering its eye by expanding or contracting a lobe of skin over the pupil.

◀ The Clown Loach (*Botia macracanthus*) is an endearing fish which must be kept in shoals.

The Clown Loach *(Botia macracantha)*
This smart orange and black striped fish has very tiny scales, so much so that it appears to be naked. Under the eye, it has an erectile spine which is usually raised in defence; you should take care that it does not become lodged in the net when you are catching this extremely fast-moving fish – if you ever manage to do so. The Clown Loach is very 'sociable' and should always be kept in small shoals. However, because they are quite large – 17.5 cm (7 in) long – and need to be kept in a group, they are impractical for small aquaria. Fish in this genus (and other 'naked' species) may be irritated by the chemicals in some remedies due to their skin being less protected than more 'scaly' species.

Stocking your aquarium

There are a great number of ways in which you can stock and furnish your aquarium. The vital things to remember are to choose fish that are mutually compatible and not to overstock your tank. Three schemes are suggested here which would make a well-balanced aquarium and which would provide both a congenial environment for the fish and an attractive moving picture of colour and light. All the schemes listed here are based on using a tank measuring 60 x 38 x 30 cm (24 x 15 x 12 in).

Scheme 1

This stocking scheme is suitable for a tank used in a hard and alkaline water area.

Fish

5 Tiger Barbs (*Barbus tetrazona*)
2 pairs Black Mollies (*Poecilia sphenops*)
2 pairs Guppies (*Poecilia reticulata*)
1 pair Swordtails (*Xiphophorus helleri*)
1 pair Pearl Gourami (*Trichogaster leeri*)
2–3 Corydoras (*Corydoras aeneus or paleatus*)
2 pairs Platies (*Xiphophorus maculatus*)
2 small Angelfish (*Pterophyllum scalare*)

Plants

You should select plants of varying heights (with the tallest at the back and the shortest in the front). Approximately two dozen would be a good number, although this will depend on how much other tank decoration, such as rocks, stones, bogwood, etc., you include. Choose from any of the plants listed below:
Echinodorus paniculatus (Amazon Swordplant)
Sagittaria
Vallisneria
Ludwigia (Swamp Loosestrife)
Hygrophila

◀ Angelfish (*Pterophyllum scalare*)

Scheme 2

This is suitable for a tank in an area of less hard water than referred to in Scheme 1.

Fish

5 Tiger Barbs (*Barbus tetrazona*)
5 Cardinal Tetras (*Paracheirodon axelrodi*)
5 Glowlight Tetras (*Hemigrammus erythrozonus*)
2 pairs Guppies (*Poecilia reticulata*)
1 pair Pearl Gourami (*Trichogaster leeri*)
2 Corydoras (*Corydoras aeneus or paleatus*)
2 pairs Ruby Barb (*Barbus nigrofasciatus*)
2 small Angelfish (*Petrophyllum scalare*)
5 Zebra Danios (*Brachydanio rerio*)

▲ Cardinal Tetras (*Paracheirodon axelrodi*)

▼ Ruby Barb (*Barbus nigrofasciatus*)

Plants

Choose from any of the following plants, plus any from Scheme 1 which, subject to trial and error, thrive in softer water.

Cryptocorynes
Acorus
Cabomba
Ceratopteris

Scheme 3

This set-up is suitable for a tank in an area with soft water, which may have a very slightly acid quality.

Fish

5 Glass Catfish (*Kryptopterus bicirrhis*)
5 Glowlight Tetras (*Hemigrammus erythrozonus*)
1 Siamese Fighting Fish (*Betta splendens*)
2–3 Corydoras (*Corydoras aeneus or paleatus*)
1 'Plecostomus' (*Hypostomus sp.*)
3 Harlequins (*Rasbora heteromorpha*)
2 pairs Guppies (*Poecilia reticulata*)
2–3 Clown Loaches (*Botia macracantha*)

Plants

You may select any of the plants that are featured in Schemes 1 and 2, depending on the hardness of the water. However, you should be prepared for some failures.

Aquaria

Tank size

Aquaria come in a wide range of types and designs, to suit all tastes and pockets. They are made in various combinations of materials, such as perspex or glass, with or without iron frames. The lightest modern aquaria are made of glass which is sealed with silicone glue.

Do remember that a tank full of water is extremely heavy, so it is very important to make sure that the bottom of even a lightweight aquarium is always fully supported on a firm base.

Unless you need an aquarium for a specialized purpose, such as an infirmary or as a rearing or quarantine tank, never get one less than 45 cm (18 in) long, 30 cm (12 in) wide and 30 cm (12 in) deep. As a general rule, no measurement should ever be less than the depth. Bow-fronted aquaria cost a lot more than the rectangular ones and do little to enhance the quality of life for the fish.

Avoid overcrowding

To work out how many fish may be kept safely in an unaerated tank, the rule is 2.5 cm (1 in) of fish body length (excluding tails) for every 75 sq cm (12 sq in) of water surface area. Thus a 60 x 30 x 30 cm (24 x 12 x 12 in) tank has a surface area of 1800 sq cm (288 sq in) and can accommodate 60 cm (24 in) of fish. Note that the tank depth is immaterial in such calculations.

Aeration

Although aeration will greatly increase the tank's fish-holding capacity, you should never make its use an excuse to overstock the aquarium; suffocation of your fish will occur if the aerator fails.

Positioning the tank

It is best to keep an aquarium away from extremes of temperature and also out of continuous bright light, so a window sill is not a good place to site it. Look for a spot away from direct sunlight or a room heater – an alcove beside a chimney breast is often a good place.

A tank 60 cm (24 in) long and 30 cm (12 in) wide is a good size for a novice. Although a depth of water of 38 cm (14 in) makes for a more pleasing 'picture' than 30 cm (12 in) and gives the fish more swimming room, the deeper tank cannot hold any more fish as the important criterion is the amount of water surface area, which is the same for both tanks.

◀ Aquariums are sold in many shapes and sizes – a cabinet below the aquarium has the advantage of hiding equipment such as filtration units and accessories.

Home from home

When you are setting up your aquarium, you should aim, if possible, to simulate the conditions that your fish enjoy in their wild habitat. For example, shy, nocturnal fish will want some rocks to hide behind, whereas other, more adventurous fish will need plenty of open water.

Water

The water you use for filling the aquarium will vary according to the area in which you live; for instance, it may be soft or hard, acid or alkaline. Testing kits are available from specialist aquariust shops to help you check the quality of the water for hardness and for pH (the degree of acidity or alkalinity).

Chlorine levels vary, too, and these can affect your fish. Before introducing any fish to your aquarium, you must allow the water in the tank to stand for a few days so that the chlorine escapes. For some fish, rainwater is preferable. Make sure that it is collected in a clean container and, again, allow it to stand for several days before putting it into the tank. Usually, rainwater is softer than domestic water.

Remember, too, that in a heated aquarium – even one with a lid on – water constantly evaporates. Evaporation will concentrate the minerals in the water and each time you top up the tank, especially with tap water, the mineral concentration will increase. For this reason, the regular replacement of, say, 10–15 per cent of the water in the tank every two or three weeks with previously conditioned water will keep dissolved mineral content down to a safe level. A close-fitting cover-glass will also help to minimize evaporation losses and prevent condensation damage to the aquarium lighting.

Heating the aquarium

You will always need to heat your aquarium because even if you live in a warm house with efficient central heating, the average temperature will be too low for most tropical fish, which will require a constant temperature of around 24°C (72°F). You can buy either separate or combined heaters and thermostats. A simple and extremely effective arrangement is to place the heater near the filter or the air source, with the thermostat on the other side of the tank. The water current will circulate the heat and the thermostat will control it.

It is very important that you follow the manufacturer's instructions very carefully when you are wiring up the heater and the thermostat. Water and electricity are a dangerous mixture for both you and the fish. If you are unsure about any aspect of the electricity supply, you must obtain professional advice rather than attempt the job yourself.

Filter

An aerator or pump is not essential but it is useful, especially if it is combined with a filter. The filter may be a simple plastic box which is filled with filter media, through which the water is circulated by means of air from the air pump. Detritus is thereby trapped in the filter medium. A useful tip is to place a layer of activated carbon between two layers of filter media to absorb many of the organic products from fish excretion which can inhibit fish growth.

Aquascaping

You will need to put gravel in the bottom of your tank, but please wash it thoroughly first. Put the gravel in a bowl, place this under a running cold water tap and then keep stirring the gravel until the water that flows out is quite clear. Natural rocks are another attractive and useful addition to your aquarium because algae will grow on them and the fish can hide amongst them. Choose ones that are guaranteed safe for use and avoid rocks like limestone or those that contain metal ores as these can upset the chemical composition of the water (see page 24).

Water plants are essential in the well-designed aquarium (see page 28). Visually pleasing, they perform several useful functions: they put oxygen into the water; they provide cover for the fish and a surface for egg-laying; and they provide a source of food for some species.

Ventilated covers

A ventilated cover helps to maintain the temperature of the aquarium as well as providing accommodation for lighting. It also assists in keeping out dirt, dust and fumes. Fish are susceptible to certain aerosol sprays, so avoid using these in the room where the aquarium is kept.

Lighting the aquarium

For a small aquarium, an ordinary 60-watt bulb may be sufficient for illumination. However, fluorescent tube lights are now available, the gas content of which is designed specifically to produce light that is beneficial to plant growth and to enhance the colours of the fish. You should always avoid using stark bright lights, however, and remember that, in their natural state, tropical fish like subdued lighting or shade. Remember, too, that an ordinary light bulb, unlike a fluorescent tube light, will increase the water temperature. Fluorescent lights are 'cold' lights and therefore a better choice. You will need the right starter unit for the size of tube used.

Decoration and water quality

Rockwork

Apart from adding some dramatic interest to an aquarium, rocks can play important roles for the fish and fish keeper alike. Over a period of time, any carefully contoured gravel will tend to flatten out unless it is held up by pieces of rock which are buried in the gravel. Many fish will retire behind the rocks at night-time or when seeking refuge from others; during the day their places will be occupied by nocturnal species, taking their rest during tank-lit hours. Some species will even use rocks and caves as convenient and secure spawning sites.

Rocks should be chosen for their decorative value, which may include interesting strata or colour, but do not use any soft rocks that are likely to dissolve in the water e.g. limestone, nor any with metallic ore veins showing through. Rocks with a high calcium content will harden the water very quickly and they should be used only in tanks where species enjoying hard water are to be kept.

For cave-dwelling species, you can build up caves and grottoes from pieces of rock glued together with a silicone sealant. Always stand large rocks directly on the tank base buried in the gravel, as this will avoid any risk of them toppling over onto the fish.

Decoration

Although there are now many air-operated 'action-ornaments' that are available for the aquarium (and these novelties may well play an important part in attracting youngsters into the hobby), they may not represent the ideal tank decoration to the more experienced hobbyist.

▶ The Glass Catfish (*Kryptoterus bicirrhis*) is a fascinating fish as it is completely transparent apart from its spine and body organs.

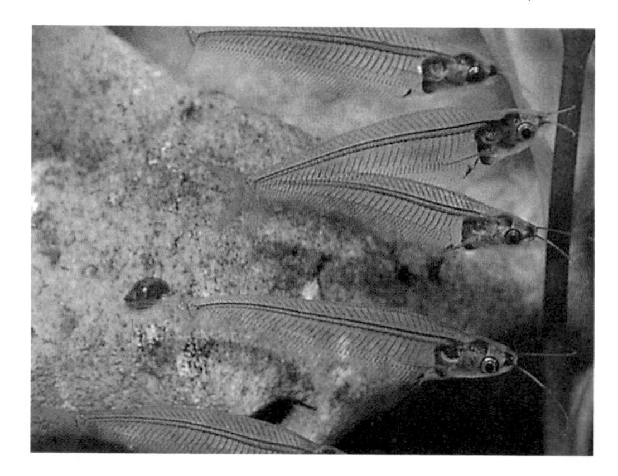

Synthetic replicas of logs and branches made from safe resin materials can look very realistic, especially when they are coated with a light layer of natural algae.

A dry diorama of rocks placed behind the aquarium and illuminated with a low-wattage lamp will add 'depth' to the aquarium when it's viewed from the front. Alternatively, a photographic underwater scene can be fixed to the outside of the aquarium at the back to give a similar effect.

◀ The Siamese Fighting Fish (*Betta splendens*) is a decorative addition, but is only suited to a quiet tank as its trailing fins can become a target for fin-nipping fish.

Water quality

As we have seen already, everything that is put into the tank will have some effect (both good and bad) upon the quality of the water. While the newcomer to fish keeping need not worry unduly about the actual water conditions (and many hobbyists keep fish in tip-top condition in blissful ignorance of such things), it may be useful to have some basic knowledge of the terms that are used in defining water quality.

The term pH is used to measure the acidity or alkalinity of the water. Distilled water is neither acidic nor alkaline and is thus referred to as being 'neutral'. The pH scale ranges from 0 to 14 (acid to alkaline) with 7, the midway mark, being the 'neutral' point. As the scale is logarithmic, an increase of 1 in either direction will represent a tenfold change in conditions.

The water may be soft or hard, depending on the amount of dissolved material in it. Thus rainwater is soft, although the degree of softness depends on how contaminated it becomes as it falls to earth and is further affected by the type of soil it subsequently flows through or over. Decaying vegetation will give the rain a soft/acid reaction, filtering through calcium-rich earth results in hard/alkaline water.

Domestic water supplies

These are treated to make them suitable for drinking but not necessarily safe for fish keeping. The removal of chlorine is made easy by the use of dechlorinators which are available from your local aquatic dealer; chlorine can also be removed by vigorous aeration. Treating tap water with a conditioner before using it in a fish tank will prevent chemical shocks, often reducing changes in pH and protecting the fishes' gills.

Aquarium equipment

Heaters and thermostats

The normal aquarium heating equipment is the internal type, with the thermostatic unit and heating element enclosed in the same watertight glass tube. Temperature adjustment is made by a control protruding through the cap. In large tanks, use two heating units (one at each end) for even distribution of heat. Separate external thermostats, either electro-mechanical or microchip-controlled, can be used with separate heaters if preferred. Allow 10 watts of 'heat' per 5 litres (1 gallon) of water: a 150-watt heater will suffice for a 54-litre (12-gallon) tank.

▼ Although a certain amount of aeration can be provided by the operation of the filter, the use of an air pump provides a stream of fine bubbles which will further enrich the aquarium environment.

Air pumps

Air pumps, in addition to providing aeration (not the necessity some novice fish keepers might think) can be put to other aquarium uses, such as driving filters and aquarium 'vacuum cleaners'. Air pumps should always be protected against water 'back-siphoning' out of the

tank by using a one-way check valve placed in the airline next to the air pump. Siting the pump above the aquarium is a more obvious answer, but as most fish keepers tend to keep their pump beside or below the aquarium, this protection is vital.

Filters

The simplest type of filter is based on a box, which is filled with various aquarium filter media, through which aquarium water is continuously passed. Suspended and dissolved matter is removed by straining or by chemical and adsorptive means. Such filters may be air- or electrically-operated. Biological filtration units (placed beneath the gravel) effect a water flow through the gravel, and encourage bacterial colonies to develop which break down toxic waste products. You must keep the filters clean so that water can pass through and they do not get clogged up.

Gravel-washers and vacuum cleaners

A gravel-washer – a very wide-necked siphoning device – can be inserted slightly into the gravel and agitated while water and detritus are removed; the heavier gravel stays behind.

Aquarium 'vacuum cleaners' are simple airlift devices, raising detritus and water from the aquarium floor and emptying them into a bag where the dirt is collected, the water returning to the tank. Battery-operated versions are available.

▼ Heater

▶ Air pumps

◀ Internal filter

▲ Lighting

Water plants

Water plants are one of the most attractive and important aspects of a well-planned aquarium. They come in many sizes and shapes, ranging from bushy growths that hide the corners of the tank, to slender, waving fronds that look pretty and give shelter for baby fish. Plants put vital oxygen into the water as well as providing food for vegetarian fish and hiding places for others. They can also help to reduce algae problems.

Water plants can sometimes be difficult to grow as certain species require specific water conditions and lighting. However, artificial water plants are also available, and these can provide some greenery in the aquarium until the live plants become established.

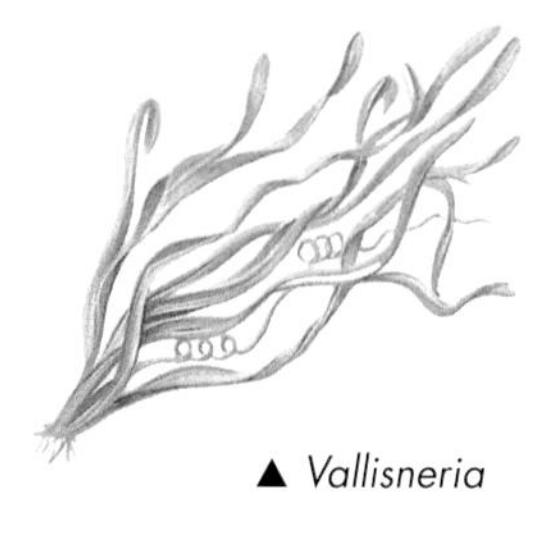

▲ *Vallisneria*

Hard water areas

Echinodorus paniculatus (Amazon Swordplant) is a popular choice. It comes in two varieties, one with narrow and one with broad leaves, and is fairly easy to propagate. *Vallisneria* is a slim-leaved plant, which is good for producing shade at the back and sides of the tank, and is found in several different varieties. *Elodea* (Canadian pondweed) grows rapidly and provides shade as well as food for some fish. *Sagittaria,* with its broad leaves, is a swift-growing plant and useful oxygenator.

▲ *Echinodorus paniculatus* (Amazon Swordplant)

Soft water areas

For areas where the water is softer, try *Cryptocoryne* species. Excellent foreground plants, they are very decorative but tend to be slow growers. They vary in size and are good where the light is weak. *Ludwigia* (Swamp Loosestrife) is often a good choice as it grows quickly, is decorative and its leaves provide useful food. *Cabomba* is another good oxygenator at the sides and back of a tank.

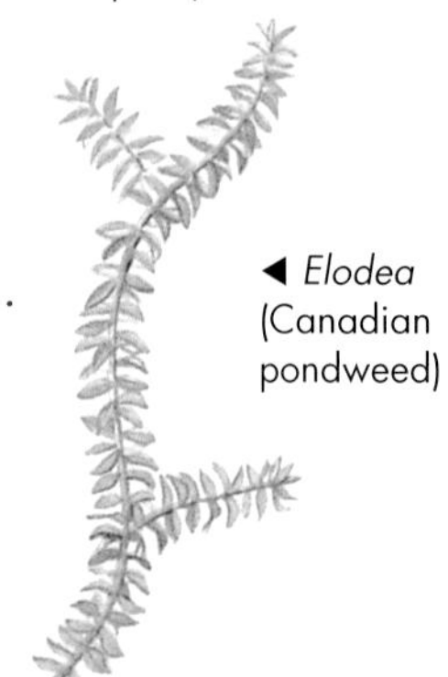

◀ *Elodea* (Canadian pondweed)

◀ *Cryptocoryne usteriana*

Root structure

Most plants have roots and therefore a suitable coarse sand or gravel (thoroughly washed) must be provided so that they can grow. Some plants, however, have a weak root structure and may be sold with a small band of lead (harmless to fish) around their bases to weight them down.

▲ Thickly planted Water Wisteria (*Hygrophlla difformis/Synnema triflorum*) provides the backdrop for these Schuberti Barbs.

◀ Despite the beautiful water plants in this well stocked aquarium, your attention will be taken most by the distinctive red snouts and striped tails of these Rummynosed Tetras (*Hemigrammus rhodostomus*).

Fitting out an aquarium

1 Always start by placing the aquarium in position on a **firm, level site**. It is a good idea to sit it on a piece of expanded polystyrene in order to cushion it against any unevenness on the base surface.

2 Put the undergravel filter in position (if this form of filter is to be used), and then add some gravel to a sloped depth of 5–8 cm (2–3 in) from the front to the back, using rocks to maintain its contour.

3 Install the thermostat/heater on the rear or side glass wall of the tank, clear of the gravel, using non-metallic clips and suction pads to fasten it in place securely.

Do not connect to the electricity supply at this stage.

4 Install the filters. Fit the airline tube and its anti-siphon valve to the air pump and then attach the other end of the airline to the input of the ganged air-valve; fit the airstone to the airline (from the ganged air-valve output) and place it in the aquarium or down the airlift tube of the undergravel filter. You can use larger rocks and water plants to hide all this aquarium 'hardware'.

5 Fill the aquarium to within 5 cm (2 in) of the top with water. Avoid disturbing the gravel by pouring the water on to a saucer or piece of expanded polystyrene to disperse the flow.

6 Root the water plants in clumps of gravel, starting with the rear and sides using tall 'grassy' plants. Fill in the corners of the tank with some bushier types. Plant smaller species on the open area of gravel near the front glass, and single larger plants further back.

7 Fill the tank to its final level, then place the cover-glass, hood and the thermometer in position. You can cut the hood and the cover-glass to accommodate any tubes and airlines where necessary.

8 Connect the wires from the lamps, thermostat/heater, filters and air pump to 'cable tidy'. Fit the plug and switch on the power. Adjust the airflow from the airstone and water flow from filters as needed. The water will probably reach the required temperature in a couple of hours.

Home aquarium checklist

1. Before you set up your home aquarium and make any expensive acquisitions, you should talk to expert aquarists and get some ideas and advice.
2. Decide on the site, size, content and cost of your tank. Be realistic and don't opt for a system that you can't afford to run or won't have the time to look after.
3. Investigate different heating and lighting systems.
4. Purchase the tank, stand, cover, heater, thermostat, thermometer, gravel and water plants, etc.
5. Thoroughly wash the gravel under running cold water until it runs completely clear.
6. Clean the tank thoroughly inside and out and position it in its permanent site – not a sunny window sill.
7. Place biological (undergravel) filter (if it is to be used) in the tank, fully covering the base. Add the washed gravel.
8. Fix the thermostat/heater (following the manufacturer's instructions carefully), and the airstone and internal/external filters (if used) in position.
9. Add some rocks and other decorations. Fill the tank almost to the top. Add the plants and complete aquascaping.
10. Completely fill the tank, leaving some air space beneath the cover-glass. Add the thermometer.
11. Connect the heating system, air pump and any electrically operated filters to the mains. Switch on.
12. Add the cover and check the lights.
13. Leave the tank for at least one week before adding any fish. During this time, make daily temperature checks and keep an eye out for leaks.
14. Buy your fish. Make absolutely sure that the ones you have chosen are compatible with one another.
15. Finally, add your fish to the tank.

Picking out healthy stock

It is extremely important to start off with healthy stock, otherwise your fish will be very short-lived. The standard of supplies of live fish varies enormously, so if possible talk to some experienced aquarists and get their advice on who are the best suppliers in your area.

As a general rule, a shop that sells only fish is more likely to be a better choice than one that sells all kinds of pets. The size of the shop is immaterial: some very small establishments may keep fish that are healthier and better-quarantined than much larger places. A shop that specifically states that all its fish are quarantined is better than one that does not. Look especially for tanks labelled 'Not for Sale – Fish in Quarantine'. This means, hopefully, that any diseases imported with the fish will not be present in those finally sold to the customer.

Sometimes, however, in less reputable fish emporia, you may find such notices on some of the aquaria but also notice that the water is continually transferring from one tank to the next, thereby transferring any ailments throughout the entire stock. So use your eyes and take advice.

Healthy fish

Once you have chosen your supplier, look at the other inmates of the tanks that contain the fish you want: if there are any unhealthy fish or the tank is very dirty, do not buy, even if your particular choice of fish looks quite unaffected – there is a risk that you will take disease home with it and thereby infect your other fish. A healthy fish will be active (except the nocturnal and naturally sedentary species) with erect fins and smooth skin. Avoid misshapen fish or ones behaving abnormally.

One final warning: many diseased fish do not show obvious signs of illness, so, especially if you are introducing new fish into an already established aquarium of healthy fish, keep the newcomers separate for a while. Despite all precautions, experience dictates that you should prepare yourself for deaths, although hopefully these will be few.

Investigate before you buy

Because different species require different conditions, you need to know exactly what you want, and what their requirements are, before you decide which fish to buy. Moreover, unless you are quite sure that you have a male and female of the same species, you will never, of course, get them to breed. Information on distinguishing males from females is given on page 44.

It is also important to remember that some fish grow to be much bigger than others (so you will want fewer of them); some large fish will eat smaller ones (quickly reducing your fish population); and the males of certain species will fight endlessly if they live together in an aquarium. Some fish prefer to live in small groups whereas others are territorial and will threaten the other fish in the tank. Obviously, the larger the aquarium, the greater the number of species of fish that you can keep, but don't be tempted to fill your tank with fish that may look good but which will not get along together. If you are a beginner with no previous experience of fish keeping, it is probably best to start with those fish that are the easiest to keep and the least expensive to buy.

Know your fish families

Just to add to the newcomer's confusion, in addition to their classified scientific names, most tropical freshwater fish have common names bestowed upon them by hobbyists and dealers alike. This is all very well, until more than one common name is used for the same species. Different dealers may refer to *Xenocara dolichoptera*, for example, as the Flag Cat, Blue Chin or Guyanan Blue Fin, which can lead to confusion. Or a common name, such as the Red-tailed Black Shark or Chinese Sucking 'Loach', may be deceptive.

By far the best knowledge that you can acquire in respect of fish families is to know to which group each fish belongs, then you will be in a far better position to provide for its needs in the aquarium, and also to understand how it fits in (or not) with other species that you might want to add to your collection. The challenge of breeding fish will again require you to get to know more about fish families, as they do not all breed in the same manner, and a little advance knowledge is always better than hindsight where livestock is concerned. The golden rule is 'always put the fish's interests first'.

▼ One of the main attractions of fishkeeping is that you can set the levels of attainment yourself. You may be quite content with a simple community collection or you may venture further and maintain a tank of such exotic species as these unusual *Discus*, or Pompadour Fish, which are more suited for the experienced aquarist.

The healthy tropical fish

Different species of tropical fish require different conditions – both of temperature and habitat. However, there are certain common rules that apply to them all and it is sensible to observe your fish regularly.

Signs of health

Appetite	Good, with food eaten swiftly and enthusiastically.
Breathing	The gill covers should rise and fall rhythmically; gulping at the surface (except in the case of Labyrinth Fish, Loaches and some Catfish) indicates oxygen starvation.
Demeanour	Should be alert; one fish that leaves the rest of its shoal to be by itself may be sick.
Eyes	These are usually bright and clear.
Fins	They should be entire, without tears, splits, white spot or streaks of blood; should be held away from the body; not drooping or folded.
Position in water	Swimming freely; sick fish may sink to the bottom or float on the surface on their side (though Catfish especially often adopt seemingly odd positions).
Scales	Scales should show no injury or fungal growth; protruding scales are a sign of disease.
Vent	Should be clean with no trailing faeces.

General signs of unhealthiness

These include: sunken bellies; protruding scales; listlessness (except in some retiring or nocturnal fish); discoloured patches on the skin; ragged fins; white spots; white strands like cottonwool; milky eyes (where applicable); irregular swimming or an irregular position (though some Catfish naturally rest at 'peculiar' angles).

Settling in your fish

Getting the aquarium ready

Once you have set up your aquarium in its permanent position, planted your water plants, added decorations and completed the aquascaping, and also tested out your heating, lighting and filtration system, it is advisable to wait for a week or two before you introduce your fish. This will give the plants a chance to get established and will enable the water to 'age' as well as offering you the opportunity to make sure that everything is working just as it should. It is normal to be eager to fill up the aquarium with your long-awaited fish but you should err on the side of caution and be prepared to wait a little while longer.

Bringing your fish home

Having purchased your fish, the next step is to bring them home safely. They will most likely be sold in plastic bags, so if you have a long journey, ask the shop assistant to put the plastic bags in a polystyrene container so that the temperature loss is kept to a minimum. Normally the supplier will ensure that enough air is contained above the water in each bag for the fish to survive; the bag must contain slightly more air than water, and the fish should not be crowded.

Introducing the fish to your aquarium

It is important to remember that a tropical fish cannot adapt to any sudden changes in temperature, and therefore you need to make sure that the temperature of the water in the plastic bag containing your fish is equal to that in the aquarium. When you get home, leave the fish inside the bag in the tank for an hour or two in order to equalize the water temperatures. Turn the aquarium lighting off, as the bag might accidentally touch the bulb and melt, causing problems. Also, the fish will be calmer in the dark. They may be nervous and upset after the experience of being caught and transported, so when the moment comes for their release, slowly undo or cut open the bag and let them swim out of their own accord.

You might find it best to keep the aquarium lights off to begin with while the fish settle in to their new home and explore their surroundings. After a little while, you can turn the lights on again and then feed the newcomers. Healthy fish enjoy eating, so being given a meal after what has been for them a traumatic experience, can help to settle them down and encourage them to associate their new environment with a regular supply of food.

Feeding

▲ Water fleas (*Daphnia*)

Fish soon learn about food. If you feed them, say, at about 7pm every evening, before that time they will be waiting below the spot at which food is introduced. Regular times for meals are a sensible idea for you and the fish.

A well-balanced diet

Most of the proprietary flake foods will be suitable for almost all fish. They have the advantage of containing the appropriate amounts of minerals, vitamins, fats and fibres, and they are also convenient to dispense. You will need to judge the quantity carefully for yourself, but as a general rule of thumb don't give fish more food than they can eat in a couple of minutes. It is better to feed a little and often rather than too much at one go. Excess food is not always eaten later; it pollutes the water, increasing the bacteria content and subsequent risk of disease.

Live foods are always beneficial

The most commonly available live foods are small crustaceans called *Daphnia*, or water fleas, which can be put into the tank straight away. You can also get live blood worms (the larvae of mosquito-like insects) and *Tubifex* worms. Be wary of *Tubifex* worms, however, as although they are good and nutritious food, they live half-buried in possibly disease-carrying mud, in foul waters with a low oxygen content.

Household foods can be included

A few ordinary household foods are good for fish, but always give them in small quantities mixed with proprietary brands. Finely chopped lean meat and ground fish are worth adding to the diet, and so are

◀ Keep *Tubifex* worms in a bowl under a trickling cold tap for at least three days before you feed them to your fish. Without the mud they knot their bodies into a ball, so you will lose only the dead ones, and the process will rid the rest of diseases that they may be carrying.

ground porridge oats and some of the invalid foods that are formulated for humans. Very small fish (newly born young or dwarf species) will benefit from small quantities of finely crumbled-up hard-boiled egg yolks. Vegetarian fish will appreciate small pieces of lettuce leaf.

Correct feeding

Not only are the quantity, quality and size of the food that you offer important but also how it is given. Earlier in this book (see page 10), fish were described as surface, middle-, or bottom-feeding species, and their foods should be presented accordingly. Long-floating flake foods will satisfy the surface-feeders, but the mid- and bottom feeders will need food that sinks more quickly. Nocturnal species, such as Catfish, should always be fed last thing at night. However, some fish keepers mistakenly treat them as scavengers and expect them to clear up any uneaten food left by the other fish.

◀ As an alternative to flake food, tablets of compressed food can be stuck to the aquarium glass for the fish to peck at. These young Platies seem to find it irresistible.

Maintenance and handling

The well-run aquarium

A well-established aquarium will almost run itself; food and light are the only 'fuels' that are needed to keep it going. One important daily check is to count the fish: you should notice their general condition and be on the look-out for any abnormalities in their swimming actions or behaviour. Absentees may be hiding behind rocks or even on the floor of the tank. Always remove any dead fish to prevent spread of disease.

Scrape off excess algae from time to time, taking care not to scratch the sides of plastic tanks when doing so. Even the most efficient filter must be periodically cleaned, otherwise toxins in the collected detritus may dissolve back into the constantly passing aquarium water.

Fast-growing plants may be pruned back to encourage 'bushing-out' and to provide extra stock. Remove any dead or dying leaves. The regular removal of, say, 10–15 per cent of the water is recommended practice in order to ensure that the mineral content of the water does not become excessively high and also to help cut down the amount of any dissolved waste products. Siphoning off the water from the bottom removes detritus in the process. Replace lost water with dechlorinated water of approximately the same temperature.

Stripping down the tank

If a whole strip-down is needed then the first thing to do is *switch off the electricity*. Siphon off some aquarium water into a container (a large covered bowl or a spare tank) and, using a net, place the fish inside it. Remove the aquarium plants and hardware and put them to one side in a safe place. Siphon out the rest of the water and remove any rocks and gravel. *Never attempt to carry the tank with water and/or rocks and gravel in it.* Apart from risking personal injury, it's almost impossible and the bottom glass may easily crack. Rinse the gravel clean and scrub the rocks. Thoroughly clean out the tank with fresh water. Using dechlorinated water if possible, refurnish the tank (as described on page 30). Once the water temperature is correct, re-introduce the fish. Clean the cover-glass and replace the light bulbs or fluorescent light as necessary.

Safe and sensible handling

Fish are delicate and sensitive creatures. Careless handling can easily hurt them, and so can abrupt changes in temperature or light and strong vibrations, like sudden loud noises or tapping on the side of the tank.

In general, fish must not be handled with your bare hands at all. If you must move them to temporary accommodation, it is best to use a net to catch them. In these circumstances, do remember to equalize the water temperature as outlined on page 35.

It is not a good idea to plunge fish abruptly from bright light into sudden darkness or vice versa. If your aquarium is lit, try to remember to turn the light off before the room lights at night, so as to make the transition to darkness gentler and more gradual for the fish.

Should you need to transfer the aquarium to a new home, try to take as much of the original aquarium water with you as possible; this will lessen the shock of the transfer. If the journey is long, transport the fish in an insulated container – a polystyrene box is ideal. If the tank is small – up to 60 cm (24 in) long – leave the gravel in during transit, but remove the rocks, which might topple and break a glass panel.

Netting fish

Try to catch fish as gently as possible when netting. Use a second smaller net to guide the fish into a larger one – this is better than chasing a terrified fish all around the aquarium with a single net.

◀ Great care is required when netting tropical fish; soft nylon nets with a fine mesh size will prevent damage to fins.

Ailments

Fish ailments and diseases are very hard to diagnose as superficially similar symptoms may be caused by many different infections. Bacteria, fungi, viruses, protozoa (single-celled organisms) and helminths (internal parasites or worms) can all affect fish, as can adverse environmental factors, over which we may have a certain degree of control.

Too rapid temperature change

If a tropical fish is suddenly placed in water that is too cold, it will go into a state of shock (as it will if the tank heater or thermostat fails). This is manifested by a slow, weaving style of swimming – often called shimmying. Too rapid a rise in temperature will cause a shortage of oxygen in the water so that the fish will gasp for breath at the surface.

Poisons

Many of the heavy metals are poisonous to tropical fish. Of these, the worst is copper, so you must avoid having any copper in contact with aquarium water. Zinc can also be lethal. Lead, although a poison, is less of a problem (for instance, if used to weight down aquatic plants) because it rapidly becomes covered by a layer of inert lead oxide. Other ordinary substances are harmful to fish health. For instance, aerosol sprays should not be used in close proximity to the aquarium, and insecticides can be lethal.

If the water in your aquarium becomes toxic, you must change 50 per cent of the water as soon as possible. Always make sure that you use dechlorinated tap water at the same temperature as the water in the tank. Keep doing 30 per cent water changes until the water tests negative for ammonia and nitrate and the fish appear normal.

Bad feeding

Complaints due to incorrect feeding may not appear immediately, and by the time that something is seen to be wrong, it may already be too late to remedy it. Too much of one type of food can cause intestinal trouble – flake food, however, is mixed and therefore a good option. However, too much fat and carbohydrate in the fish's diet can lead to the degeneration of the digestive organs and the deposition of unhealthy fat. Should your fish persistently have long strings of faeces, something is wrong. You should try changing the diet and seek expert advice if things do not improve.

White spot disease

This is one of the complaints that fish suffer from which is, to some extent, outside your control. It is a fairly common disease which is caused by protozoa. The skin of the fish becomes covered by small white spots about the size of a pin head. The damaging organism is called *Ichthyophthirius*, which is often abbreviated to 'ich'. Ich matures in the skin of the fish where it feeds on skin cells. It then leaves the fish and reproduces. The hundreds of young in their turn feed on the fish, thereby continuing the cycle.

As white spot can only be treated effectively when the parasite is free-swimming, you must treat the whole aquarium. Remedies are available from aquarist shops and you must complete the course of treatment. Quarantine any new fish before introducing them to the tank.

Fungus

Fungus is a general term for several different infections that show up as cotton-wool-like strands on the fish's body, fins and gills. If it is left untreated, fungus can be fatal. The spores, which are often present in fish tanks, will attack damaged or sick fish, with the fungal growths spreading to vulnerable areas, such as the eyes and gills. The similar-looking Mouth Fungus is a quite different disease and will not respond to the same treatments, although antibiotics are effective.

Basic treatment for sick fish

You should always isolate any suspect fish as quickly as possible in order to avoid the spread of disease. You can either transfer it to a separate aquarium (a sick tank or an infirmary) or float a jam jar of aquarium water in the aquarium with the patient inside it.

Treatments for white spot, fungus and many other diseases are available from good aquarium shops, but do not expect universal success. There is nothing wrong with many of the medicaments: the problem is that similar symptoms can arise from different causes.

There are various chemicals available that can prevent many diseases, but you would be well advised to read widely before using them as, incorrectly applied, they can do more harm than good.

Further advice

Fish-food and accessory manufacturers usually offer excellent advisory services, and answers to many aquatic troubles appear in the 'problem pages' of hobby magazines. However, if you need urgent help with diagnosing and treating diseases – some spread very quickly – you should contact your dealer, local aquarist society or a veterinary surgeon who specializes in treating tropical fish.

Reproduction

How fish breed

All fish develop from eggs but there are two distinct methods of doing so: the majority of fish lay eggs that are fertilized externally, from which the young hatch out after a period of hours, days or months, depending on the species. Other fish, which are known as live-bearers, develop internally fertilized eggs within the female's body from where they emerge as free-swimming miniature replicas of their parents. Live-bearing fish provide the aquarist with the raw material for selective breeding, and this is how all the colourful cultivated strains are made available.

Male live-bearing fish can be identified easily by their rod-shaped, or notched, anal fin; male fish of egg-laying species are slimmer and much more brightly coloured than the females.

Breeding conditions

It is very important to realize that different species, as well as being either egg-laying or live-bearing, require different conditions if they are to breed successfully. Therefore, in a mixed aquarium, the breeding environment that might suit a Guppy, for instance, can be quite inappropriate for, say, a Gourami.

Egg-laying species

Whereas live-bearing fish young can survive in a heavily weeded community tank without any extra precautions, the egg-laying species will require a multitude of different habitats: some scatter their eggs over gravel, into which they fall and subsequently develop unattended by their parents, while others, such as Labyrinth Fish – Gouramis and Siamese Fighting Fish – make bubble nests at the surface and protect them and the young carefully. Some Cichlids and Catfish lay sticky eggs on to rocks or plants and may or may not (depending on the species) look after the eggs and/or young, while other Cichlids excavate nests for their eggs in the sand or gravel.

Raising maximum young

It is important to remember that in the wild only a very small proportion of the fry born actally reach adulthood. This is substantially true in home aquarium conditions, too, as many of the young fry are eaten by other fish, including, very often, their own parents. In order to raise the maximum number of young, therefore, it may be necessary to isolate them from the other fish, either by using a separate nursery tank or by putting a divider or partition into your existing aquarium.

Specialized knowledge

As you will by now appreciate, tropical fish breeding is a relatively complex business and it should never be entered into lightly. If you are intent on breeding your fish, then it is strongly recommended that you consult a number of experienced fish breeders and read a variety of reference books on the subject before embarking on a breeding programme in order to gain more information and guidance.

▲ Cichlids guard their young carefully.

Your questions answered

What measures should be taken during power cuts?

The water temperature will fall quite slowly, more so in larger tanks, and a few hours will need to pass before a dangerously low level is reached. If a prolonged power loss is anticipated, particularly in the winter months, then the water temperature can be maintained by standing bottles of hot water (heated by alternative means) in the aquarium.

Why do my fish scratch about on the rocks?

They may be infested with a skin parasite which they are attempting to dislodge by their scratching actions. If your fish are doing this, seek advice immediately from an experienced aquarist, vet or your dealer for an accurate diagnosis. The condition is quite curable.

How can I tell whether my fish are males or females?

Most male live-bearers have a rod-shaped anal fin; females have the normal fan-shaped fin. Males of egg-laying species are slimmer, more brightly coloured and have longer fins than the females, which are plumper, a condition more easily seen from above.

How should fish be looked after in my absence?

Healthy, well-fed fish can generally be left to their own devices for up to two weeks. Giving a non-fishkeeping neighbour the task of feeding them, however, may result in overfeeding unless small pre-packed meals are left, together with instructions on how to feed them. You can also purchase a 'vacation feeder', which releases small food particles gradually over a period of time. However, even if you are using one of these, a responsible person should still be asked to check the tank daily to ensure that the electrical equipment is working properly.

Why are partial water changes necessary if a filter is fitted?

Not all filters remove dissolved water products totally. Changing some of the aquarium water regularly helps keep down the levels of dissolved wastes and ensures that trace elements are kept at optimum levels.

How often should I clean out the filter?

This all depends on how dirty the aquarium is; rinsing the filter medium (in aquarium water) once every two to three weeks will lengthen its life for a while; any lessening water flow from filters indicates that cleaning out has been left too long and too late!

My Catfish often dash to the surface and gulp air. Is the aquarium lacking in oxygen?

No. Catfish use air gulped at the surface as an alternative to breathing dissolved oxygen; it is absorbed into their blood in their gut.

My fish have begun to hang at the surface, gasping for air. What is wrong?

There is insufficient oxygen in the water or they cannot make use of what is available. Increase aeration – the pump may have stopped, the tank may be overcrowded or there may be decaying matter on the tank floor. Check for inflamed gills and increased breathing rates, which may be due to a parasitic infection of the gills; if so, seek qualified help.

How can I get my plants to grow and thrive?

Many variables affect healthy plant growth. These include the amount of light, depth of gravel and which plants you grow together. Like fish, not all plants are compatible, and many houseplants that are sold as being aquarium-suitable simply are not. Another reason may be the use of undergravel filters but this is a contentious point amongst aquarists.

Shortly after setting up my aquarium, the water turned misty. Will it clear or should I start again?

You must always remember that the aquarium is a collection of many living things – not just the fish and the water plants within it. There is quite likely to be a rapid development of bacteria and minute algae spores in the water which will produce a misty or cloudy effect until the plants become well established and the aquarium reaches some point of natural balance. Modern filters will help to keep cloudiness at bay (it may only be dirt stirred up by fish, after all) and you can do likewise by carrying out regular partial water changes (see page 22) and never overfeeding (see page 36), as any 'leftover' food will contribute to the water pollution.

Index